Instrumentation

The accompaniment to this work exists in three versions:

1. For chamber orchestra (2 flutes (1 doubling piccolo), 2 oboes, bassoon, 2 horns, harp and percussion (1 player), and strings).

2. For organ, brass quintet (2 trumpets in B♭, horn in F, trombone, and tuba), and percussion (1 player).

3. For organ alone. The organist plays from the vocal score.

Full scores and instrumental parts for versions 1 and 2 are available on hire from the publisher. Please specify, when ordering, which version is required.

Duration: 15 minutes

Composer's Note

I have always loved Christmas and the carols we sing at that special time of year, and I wrote the cantata *Christus Natus Est* in response to a commission from conductor George Vass. The work takes the form of a sequence of five Christmas carols: *Personent hodie*; *Entre le bœuf et l'âne gris*; *Gaudete!*; *Infant holy, Infant lowly*; and *Angelus ad Virginem*. I have made use of a motif from one of my own original carols, *Of a Rose*, to give an instrumental introduction and as linking material between each section.

Christus Natus Est was first performed by the St Albans Choral Society, the Choir of St Hilda's School, Harpenden, and Orchestra Nova, conducted by George Vass, on 8 December 2002 at the Alban Arena, St Albans. It has been recorded by soprano Rachel Nicholls, the City of Canterbury Chamber Choir, Parmiter's Senior Singers, and Orchestra Nova, conducted by George Vass, on Dutton Epoch CDLX 7146.

Christus Natus Est

A Cantata for Christmas

CECILIA McDOWALL

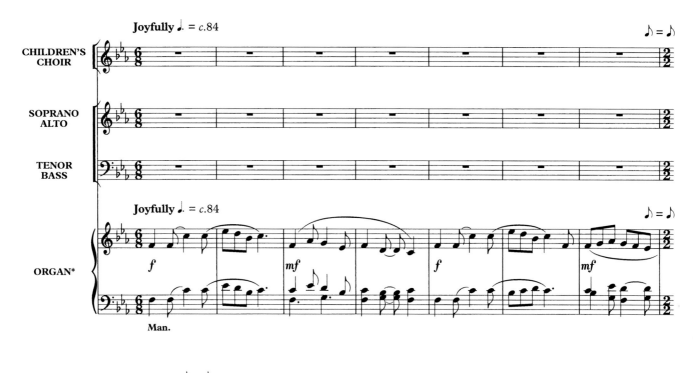

* This part may also be played on the piano.

Printed in Great Britain

OXFORD UNIVERSITY PRESS, MUSIC DEPARTMENT, GREAT CLARENDON STREET, OXFORD OX2 6DP

OXFORD

Christus Natus Est

A Cantata for Christmas

Cecilia McDowall

MUSIC DEPARTMENT

OXFORD

UNIVERSITY PRESS

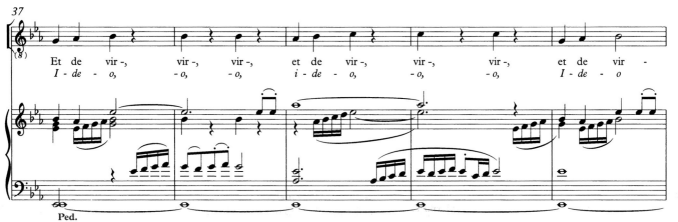

8

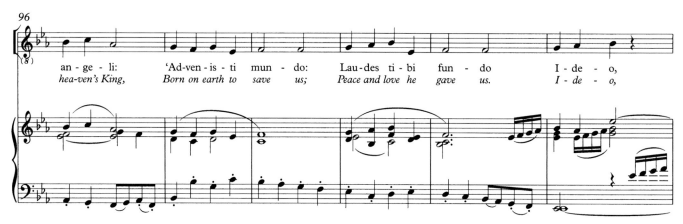

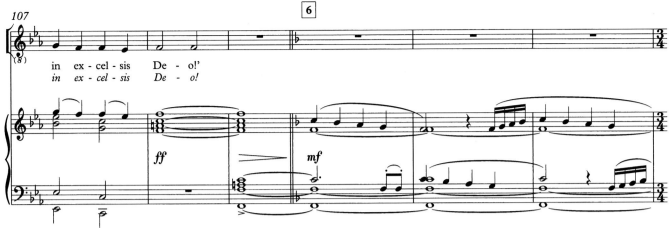

Vo-lent à l'en-tour De ce Dieu d'a-mour.
Round the God of Love in the man - ger here.

ah

ah

12 Joyfully ♩. = c.84

16

225

T.B.

De-us ho-mo fac-tus est, Na-tu-ra mi-ran - te; Mun-dus re-no - va-tus est A Chris-to reg-nan - te.

233 *f unis.*

S.A.

Gau-de-te! gau-de-te! Chris-tus est na-tus Ex Ma-ri-a Vir-gi-ne: gau-de-te! E-

T.B.

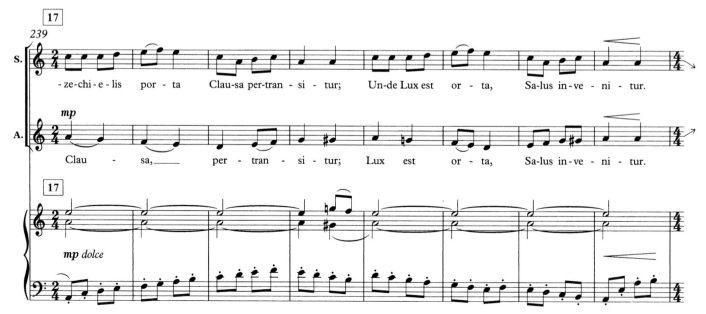

17

239

S.

-ze-chi-e-lis por-ta Clau-sa per-tran-si-tur; Un-de Lux est or-ta, Sa-lus in-ve-ni-tur.

A.

Clau - sa, ___ per-tran-si-tur; Lux est or-ta, Sa-lus in-ve-ni-tur.

18

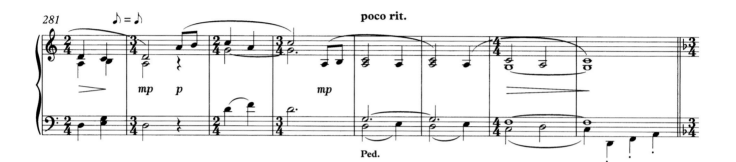

303

ring-ing, ti-dings bring-ing: Christ the Babe is Lord of all, Christ the Babe is Lord of all.

mf dolce

Ped.

310 22

p

2. Flocks were sleep-ing, shep-herds keep-ing Vi-gil till the morn-ing new; Saw the

Man.

316

glo-ry, heard the sto-ry, Ti-dings of a gos-pel true. Thus re-joic-ing, free from sor-row, Prai-ses

Ped.

322

voi-cing, greet the mor-row: Christ the Babe was born for you, Christ the Babe was born for you.

Sw. Solo

Man. Ped.

26

L'istesso tempo

ALL VOICES (not CHILDREN'S CHOIR)

388

1. An - ge - lus ad Vir - gi - nem Sub - in - trans in___ con - cla - ve,
1. Ga - bri - el to Ma - ry came, And en - tered at___ her dwell - ing,

394

Vir - gi - nis for - mi - di - nem De - mul - cens, in - quit, 'A - ve! A - ve Re - gi - na Vir - gi - num!
With his sal - u - ta - tion glad Her mai - den fears dis - pel - ling, 'All hail, thou queen of vir - gins bright!

400

Ce - li Ter - re - que Do - mi - num Con - ci - pi - es, Et pa - ri - es___ In - tac - ta Sa -
God, Lord of earth and hea - ven's height, Thy___ ve - ry Son, Shall soon be born___ in pure - ness, The

406

-lu - tem ho - mi - num; Tu___ Por - ta ce - li fac - ta, Me - de - la Cri - mi - num.'
Sa - viour of___ man - kind. Thou art the gate___ of hea - ven bright, The sin - ners' heal - er kind.'

Ped.

+32'

Christus Natus Est

A Cantata for Christmas

CECILIA McDOWALL

* Children's choir tacet until bar 289.

This page may be photocopied

Printed in Great Britain

OXFORD UNIVERSITY PRESS, MUSIC DEPARTMENT, GREAT CLARENDON STREET, OXFORD OX2 6DP

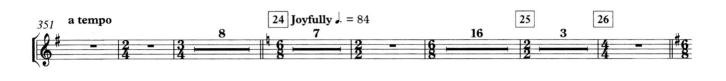

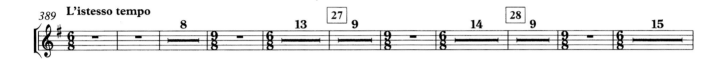

4. E - ya, Ma - ter Do - mi - ni, Que pa - cem red - di - di - sti An - ge - lis et ho - mi - ni Cum
4. Hail! thou Mo - ther of the Lord, Who brings't of gifts the ra - rest, Peace to ang - els and to men, When

Chris-tum ge - nu - i - sti, Tu - um ex - o - ra Fil - li - um Ut se no - bis pro-pi - ci - um Ex -
Christ the Lord thou ba - rest! Do thou, we pray, en - treat thy Son For us our long'd re - demp - ti - on Him -

-hi - be - at Et de - le - at Pec - ca - ta, Pre-stans aux - i - li - um Vi - ta fru - i - be - a - ta, Post
-self to win, And from our sin Re - lease us; his suc - cour for to give, That, when we hence are ta - ken, We

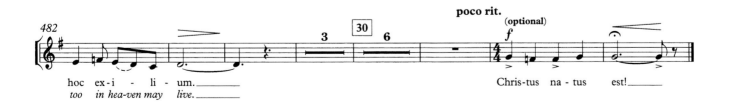

hoc ex - i - li - um. Chris-tus na - tus est!
too in hea-ven may live.

Music origination by Barnes Music Engraving Ltd., East Sussex
Printed by Halstan and Co. Ltd., Amersham, Bucks., England

OXFORD CAROLS

Oxford publishes a vast array of Christmas music to suit every occasion and choir. There are pieces and collections for services, concerts, and carol-singing; pieces for SATB, upper-voice, and unison choirs; *a cappella* carols and carols with piano or organ accompaniment; and a wealth of traditional favourites alongside new carols by leading composers. There are also over 250 orchestrations of carols from *Carols for Choirs* and other collections available for hire, including versions for brass, strings, and full orchestra. With hundreds of individual titles and an impressive range of carol anthologies, Oxford provides a rich collection of the very best in Christmas music.

Selected carol anthologies from Oxford University Press

For Him all Stars, 15 carols for upper voices

Gaudete! 10 carols for mixed voices, arranged by Bob Chilcott

A Merry Little Christmas, 12 popular classics for choirs
Compiled and edited by Jerry Rubino

An Edwardian Carol Book, 12 carols for mixed voices
Selected and edited by Jeremy Dibble

Bob Chilcott Carols, 9 carols for mixed voices

John Rutter Carols, 10 carols for mixed voices

Mack Wilberg Carols, 8 carols for mixed voices

World Carols for Choirs, SATB and upper-voice editions
Compiled and edited by Bob Chilcott and Susan Knight

Christmas Spirituals for Choirs
Compiled and edited by Bob Chilcott and Ken Burton

Carols for Choirs, 1–4

100 Carols for Choirs
Edited and arranged by David Willcocks and John Rutter

The Oxford Book of Carols
Edited by Percy Dearmer, Ralph Vaughan Williams, and Martin Shaw

The New Oxford Book of Carols
Edited by Hugh Keyte and Andrew Parrott

The Shorter New Oxford Book of Carols
Edited by Hugh Keyte and Andrew Parrott

UNIVERSITY PRESS

www.oup.com

ISBN 978-0-19-335893-5

9 780193 358935